A Heavenly Romance

Hidden in Plain Sight

Wayne Skinner

TEACH Services, Inc.
PUBLISHING
www.TEACHServices.com • (800) 367-1844

World rights reserved. This book or any portion thereof may not be copied or reproduced in any form or manner whatever, except as provided by law, without the written permission of the publisher, except by a reviewer who may quote brief passages in a review.

The author assumes full responsibility for the accuracy of all facts and quotations as cited in this book. The opinions expressed in this book are the author's personal views and interpretations, and do not necessarily reflect those of the publisher.

This book is provided with the understanding that the publisher is not engaged in giving spiritual, legal, medical, or other professional advice. If authoritative advice is needed, the reader should seek the counsel of a competent professional.

Copyright © 2019 Wayne Skinner
Copyright © 2019 TEACH Services, Inc.
ISBN-13: 978-1-4796-0926-0 (Paperback)
ISBN-13: 978-1-4796-0929-1 (ePub)
Library of Congress Control Number: 2019940781

All Bible text references taken from the New King James Version (NKJV) of the Bible. Copyright © 1982 by Thomas Nelson. Used by permission. All rights reserved. Emphasis added by the author of this book.

Published by

www.TEACHServices.com • (800) 367-1844

Table of Contents

Introduction. 5

"Hidden in plain sight." 7

"The Courtship" 19
(Revelation 2:7 and 11)

"Going Steady" 34
(Revelation 2:17)

"The Engagement" 51
(Revelation 2:26–28)

"The Ceremony" 60
(Revelation 3:5)

"The Marriage" 71
(Revelation 3:12, 21)

"The Beginning" 81
(1 Corinthians 2:9)

Introduction

Jesus loves you! Yes, He really does. He's madly in love with you. It's a crazy kind of love. He chose to die, rather than spend eternity without you. He thinks about you all the time. He even has a tattoo of your name on His hand. He's head-over-heels in love with you. He even writes songs about you and poems about you. He paints the evening sky with color, for you. The night sky is all shimmery with lights to remind you that He is watching over you. Rainbows appear to let you know that He hasn't forgotten you. He loves you with an unsurpassed, unfailing, unending kind of love.

And guess what?

He wants to take you on a date. Yes, the most romantic date, ever. Then He wants to get engaged—to you. Then, of course,

He wants to marry you ... yes, you. He wants you to move into His home and live with Him forever. Didn't you know that? Have you missed all of His hints, clues, and declarations? Maybe you have.

Well, there is one place in the Bible where many of us failed to see His intentions. It's been there all along. He has written a series of love notes to you ... right there in the last book of the Bible. When you put the notes together, the total message appears.

It's a spectacular message! It's written to be an invitation, and a source of encouragement. It's dripping with love. It's scented with heavenly cologne ... and it's "hidden in plain sight."

"Hidden in plain sight."

"It's hidden in plain sight." We've heard that expression before, haven't we? Here is the definition: to be unnoticeable, by staying visible in a setting that masks presence.* The phrase can be used to describe an object or a person, or in the case of this book, a love story. It is the greatest love story ever told. You'll recognize one of the

---

*http://1ref.us/qq (accessed November 5, 2018).

central figures. The other person getting married may surprise you. Of course, at the heart of every love story is romance. And…

…We all love a good romance.

The human story is full of romance. Romance is interwoven throughout the very fabric of human history. The human story is full of romance. Romance is interwoven throughout the very fabric of human history. You'll find it in every time period, culture, and location. Romance is universal.

The authors of the Bible recounted some epic romances. The stories of Adam and Eve, Abraham and Sarah, Samson and Delilah, are classic examples. Isaac and Rebekah, Jacob and Rachel, David and Bathsheba, Hosea and Gomer, are others. Some romances had positive results—and others didn't work out so well. Some romances were ordained by God and others were forbidden by God. It seems that every romantic encounter, both present and past, has or has had possibility ... possibility for ups and downs. Challenges and romances seem to go hand in hand. We have to take the good with the bad. Even in the wedding vows that we recite, the reality is expressed. "...In sickness and health, richer or poorer, in good times and bad..." Human romances are fraught with pitfalls. Maybe, that's why we love them. Maybe it's because we can identify with or long for that special someone to come into our own lives. All of the romantic tales contain the potential for drama, and *drama makes for a great story*.

There are certain phrases that we use when describing romances. How many stories have you heard which contain one or more of the following phrases?

"Love at first sight"
"Shotgun wedding"

"Puppy love"
"Star-crossed lovers"
"Unrequited love"
"Whirlwind romance"
"Life-long partners"
"Soul mates"

Whenever two human beings get together, almost anything can, and often does, happen. So maybe, that's why we love them. There is always a hint of the mysterious, and *mystery makes for a great story*.

So, it is interesting that God uses romance, with its hints of drama and the mysterious, to describe His relationship with us. In fact, it is the key way that He describes the type of relationship that He wants to have with you and me. The Bible describes several different types of relationships between God and His people. There is the analogy of the Shepherd and His flock. We read of the servant and the Master relationship. Other passages use the Parent and child relationship. Even the example of best friends is used as an illustration. But, the favorite theme of the Bible seems to be the story of lovers. Lovers destined for *a Heavenly Romance* is the overarching theme of the Good Book. In the big picture, God is seeking to restore the broken relationship between Himself and His beloved. From Genesis to Revelation (that's right—Revelation. We'll get to that in a moment …), it is the common thread that connects it all. The Good Book contains the grand story of God pursuing human beings. He is consistently wooing us. It hurts Him when we choose other "lovers." He desires to be in a loving, romantic relationship with us. He desires a romance that lasts throughout eternity.

The story of God's pursuit of humanity is, at times, heartwarming, and at other times, heartbreaking. There is betrayal, and forgiveness. There are tales of murder, separation, reunion, and many other twists and turns in the plot. No wonder we love this type of story. It's been appropriately called, "The greatest story ever told."

Now, let's get back to Revelation. The book of Revelation contains many interesting, and sometimes confusing, things. There are prophesies, beasts, seals, and trumpets. We find images of flying angels with messages, and letters to seven ancient churches. Many people find that the book of Revelation is too confusing to understand. We wonder what it all means and have a plethora of questions. Do we understand the symbolism? Why do so many people come up with so many different interpretations? Does anyone really, truly know what the strange images mean? Well … if you are looking for answers to those questions, then this is *not* the book for you. In this book, we will simply take a closer look at the conclusions to each of those seven letters. They are found in Revelation chapters 2 and 3. We will focus on the promises that God gives to *"those who overcome"* at the end of each letter. You'll be surprised to see how much they read like the ultimate romance. It is, in fact, *A Heavenly Romance*, and it's hidden in plain sight.

Are you interested? If not, put down this book and pick up something else. But, if you love a really good romance, then pull up a chair, make yourself comfortable, and keep reading.

Okay, let me share with you the portions of scripture that will be the basis of this book:

> Rev. 2:7—"He who has an ear, let him hear what the Spirit says to the churches. To him who overcomes I will give to eat from the tree of life, which is in the midst of the Paradise of God."
>
> 2:11—"…He who overcomes shall not be hurt by the second death."
>
> 2:17—"…I will give some of the hidden manna to eat. And I will give him a white stone, and on the stone a new name written which no one knows except him who receives it."

2:26—"...to him I will give power over the nations,"

2:27—"He shall rule them with a rod of iron; they shall be dashed to pieces like the potter's vessels'—as I also have received from My Father;"

2:28—"and I will give him the morning star."

Rev. 3:5—"He who overcomes shall be clothed in white garments, and I will not blot out his name from the Book of Life; but I will confess his name before My Father and before His angels."

3:12—"... I will make him a pillar in the temple of My God, and he shall go out no more. I will write on him the name of My God and the name of the city of My God, the New Jerusalem, which comes down out of heaven from My God. And I will write on him My new name."

3:21—"...I will grant to sit with Me on My throne, as I also overcame and sat down with My Father on His throne."

Do you see it? Did you catch what He is saying? Well, let me make it a bit simpler. Try this version:

My Dearest Beloved,

I am requesting that you join Me for a romantic evening. We will dine at the most exclusive restaurant in the whole universe (2:7). Once there, we will feast on the finest meal imaginable. I assure you that you will enjoy it to the fullest. The meal is so nutritious that once you eat it, you'll forever remain healthy and you will never die (2:11).

Afterwards, I will share with you a dessert treat that I have kept hidden away, just for you (2:17).

I also have a special present for you that is engraved with the pet name that I have for you. I'll tell you what it is, after we eat dessert. You're going to love it (2:17).

When we are finally together, I will give you all of the privileges and authority that are rightfully yours, as My beloved (2:26, 27).

Beloved, I truly want to share everything with you. I must tell you, that I also have a most precious rock that I want to give you. I'm so excited—I couldn't keep that to Myself any longer. The whole universe will see the brightness of this special gem (2:28).

Then, of course, I'm looking forward to our wedding ceremony. Seeing you dressed in white will thrill My heart. Our wedding will be the most viewed wedding in all of history. I will declare you to My Father and all His friends as My eternal bride. It's going to be very exciting! (3:5).

When I move you into My house, there will be a few more surprises for you. I have set everything up for you to step right in and take your rightful place. Oh, and I will personally give you a tattoo. Yes, a tattoo, that carries significant meaning (3:12).

I know I've given you a lot to think about in this letter. I am so excited! I had to share some of My thoughts and plans with you. Trust me—you don't want to miss out on any of the good things that I have planned for you. Ours will be the greatest love story ever.

> Trust me—you don't want to miss out on any of the good things that I have planned for you. Ours will be the greatest love story ever.

Eternally yours,
Jesus

I trust that the picture is becoming a bit clearer at this point. In the following chapters we will take a closer look at each of the texts and see that God has written us a stirring love letter, and indeed, it has been in plain sight this whole time. You see, it's all about love … it has always been and will always be about love.

"The Courtship"

Revelation 2:7 and 11

v. 7—"He who has an ear, let him hear what the Spirit says to the churches. To him who overcomes I will **give to eat from the tree of life, which is in the midst of the Paradise of God.**"

v. 11—"...He who overcomes shall **not be hurt by the second death.**"

Have you ever been on a blind date? You know, those dates that take place between two people who have never met face-to-face before. Maybe you've spoken over the phone, or exchanged letters, texts, and e-mail messages. But, there is nothing like that very first date. Is there anything that elicits more excitement and fear, at the same time, than a blind date? There are equal parts excitement and fear about all the possibilities. There are so many questions:

- How will they look?
- How's my hair?
- Will there be any chemistry?
- Will he/she like me?
- What if they are weird?
- What will we talk about?
- Why am I doing this, again?
- Could this be "the one"?
- Is this a good idea?

Those are some of the questions that commonly run through our minds. We sit in the parking lot waiting for the other person to show up. Wait…

… What if they don't even show up?

Have you been there? I have. I remember going on a blind date and having all of those questions and even more thoughts. As the man, one of my primary tasks was to pick the restaurant. There were a lot of choices and a ton of details to consider. The location had to be perfect. The cuisine had to have enough variety and yet be well-themed and within my price range. Ambiance was a consideration, also. I didn't want it to be too casual or too romantic, but it definitely had to be memorable. So, I did my research; I visited several establishments and made the final selection. As it turned out, it was a great choice. The evening went very well. We sat on the rooftop patio. The rays of the setting sun warmed our smiling faces. Then we capped off our well-prepared meal by sharing a delicious tiramisu. I couldn't help but feel quite pleased with myself. We had pulled off a most memorable first date.

The first date is important. The first meal together and that initial face-to-face encounter are potential signposts. They give an idea about how, and even if, the romance is going to proceed any further. We want everything to be perfect, don't we?

In Revelation 2:7 we read the following:

*"He who has an ear, let him hear what the Spirit says to the churches. To him who overcomes I will **give to eat from the tree of life, which is in the midst of the Paradise of God**."*

"The Courtship" *(Revelation 2:7 and 11)* † **23**

This is Christ talking here. We know this because He identifies Himself in the previous chapter. Revelation 1:18 reads: *"I am He who lives, and was dead, and behold, I am alive forevermore. Amen. And I have the keys of Hades and of Death."* And He is talking to you and He is talking to me. We are the ones who overcome, so the promise is for us. If we overcome then He, Jesus Christ, will treat us to a very exquisite meal. He wants to take us out to dinner. We have **been invited** to go on a date with Christ. Now, isn't that exciting?! I'm thrilled at the very thought because, on this date, He has made all the preparations. I don't have to worry about the location, the menu options, or any of those details. The price range isn't my concern, either, because He has prepaid it all.

He has taken care of all the details. He gives us a few tidbits of information about what to expect on that special, first date.

First, let's look at the venue: **"the midst of the Paradise of God."** There cannot be a better place than the Paradise of God. This is not the throne room of God or the judgment seat of God; this is the Paradise of God. It brings to mind images of the Garden of Eden, only better. God put Adam and Eve in charge of that garden and so there was the possibility of error (and we all know how that turned out). But, in the Paradise of God, God Himself is in charge.

He is the Owner, Manager, Maître D', Chef, etc. Everything is guaranteed to be perfect. The ambiance will be inviting and warm. The very atmosphere will be saturated with pure love. There will be no hint of fear, embarrassment, or unease. The sights, sounds, and fragrances will all be exquisitely prepared. It is the most exclusive eatery in the whole universe! Also, from what I understand, when you go to an exclusive restaurant, the best tables are in the center. You find those tables away from the fringes. The verse says "**...in the midst...**" Aahhh, the best possible spot has been reserved for us on this special occasion. Only the most honored guests are seated there.

No amount of money can buy a reserved table in God's Paradise. Only a select few will be welcomed there. Only those of us who overcome will be invited to dine there. Christ made the reservations some time ago, so we are sure to get in if only we accept His invitation. We will be

His special invitees; our names will be on the guest list. The heavenly hosts will be expecting us. They will await our triumphant arrival.

Now, I've never been able to make reservations at any of the exclusive restaurants here on Earth. I have never even been invited to dine at any of those locations.* So, I am looking forward to that awesome day.

Now, what about the menu? What are we going to eat? We will eat the fruit from the **"tree of life!"** We know from other passages in the Bible that this tree bears twelve different types of fruit. It bears them all at the same time, and it bears fruit every month of the year (Rev. 22:2). That's amazing, right? Even the leaves have healing qualities. Besides, we know that

---

As of the writing of this book, that is a true statement due solely to the fact that my bank account would not allow it. Maybe, by the time you are reading this book, my financial situation will have improved.

if we eat from that tree, we will live forever (Gen. 3:22). So, we will be dining on delicacies that don't exist anywhere else in the universe. The most delicious, succulent, nutritious fruit that was ever created will be presented to us. We will have up to twelve different menu options, and each one will be the most delicious thing that we have ever tasted. Unimaginable textures, smells, colors, and flavors will excite our senses like never before. The whole experience will be enhanced by the fact that we will not be overwhelmed by the variety of choices. We won't have to decide which fruit to try first, or how much to pluck from the tree. Why? Because the text says that Christ, Himself will "**…give** to eat **from the tree of life…**" He will select the fruit that He knows we will most enjoy. He will also give it to us in the quantity and sequence that will delight our palettes to the fullest. We won't have to worry about overeating or not ordering enough. "Portion control" will be up to the Savior.

Have you ever seen couples, out on a date, take turns feeding each other? Or have you been hand-fed chocolate covered strawberries by a loved one on a special occasion? Isn't it romantic? Oh, how tender will be the manner in which our Savior places the fruit in our palms. Will our fingers brush His? Oh, how sweetly He will place the morsels on our tongues. Will He caress our faces with one of His nail-scarred hands as He feeds us with the other one? Will He look lovingly into our eyes as He does so? We can only imagine. The meal, itself, will be made all the more memorable by the manner in which our loving Savior serves us. The exotic flavors of the fruit will be surpassed only by the warm glow of His loving gaze.

There is one other note about safety and security embedded in the text. Back when I was preparing for my own blind date, one of the things that I had to ponder was the safety aspect. I wanted my date to feel physically and emotionally safe. I did not want her to feel any kind of fear … no fear about getting sick from the food … no fear from the surrounding neighborhood inhabitants, or any insecurity about my intentions. I wanted her to feel totally safe in my presence. I did not want her to be hurt in any way.

In Revelation 2:11 we read the following:

> *"He, who has an ear, let him hear what the Spirit says to the churches. He who overcomes shall **not be hurt by the second death**."*

In the midst of the Paradise of God, we will feel total security. We are surrounded by the loving arms of Christ. We are in the presence of God the Father. The Holy Spirit and the host of heavenly angels encircle us. There will be no safer place in the whole universe. We will have the knowledge that the enemy of our souls, along with his sinful influences, is locked away. He will be unable to harm us, ever again. God will provide an environment where we will experience perfect peace.

> *As humans we are limited in the amount of security that we can provide ourselves or any of our loved ones. In spite of our greatest efforts and vast resources, there is nothing we can do to prevent death.*

As humans we are limited in the amount of security that we can provide ourselves

"The Courtship" *(Revelation 2:7 and 11)* † 31

or any of our loved ones. In spite of our greatest efforts and vast resources, there is nothing we can do to prevent death. The death that occurs as the natural result of sin will claim all of us if the Lord delays His return. That is called the first death and we will all be touched by it. The good news is that there is a resurrection from that death. That resurrection will result in us being reunited with our loved ones. We will meet Jesus face-to-face. So, as unsettling as the thought of the first death may be to some of us, the reality and finality of the second death really should get our knees knocking. It's that second death that results in our ultimate and eternal separation from God. It is so reassuring to dwell upon the knowledge that God promises to guard us from the second death. The fiercest enemy of humanity is rendered powerless. God pronounces that we are protected from the second death. It is then that we are truly safe. God promises that the second death will not harm us. He provides a perfect environment of peace, security, and ultimate safety.

So, for those of us who never got to meet Jesus while He walked on the Earth, that will be the most amazing blind date ever imagined! Sure, we've spoken to Him through prayer. He has spoken to us through His Word, nature, songs, and other experiences. But, this will be our first face-to-face encounter with the Savior of our souls. What an awesome first date He promises us. Every detail will be orchestrated and prepared just for us. The venue, the ambiance, the meal, and our eternal safety will have been taken into consideration. Most importantly, we will finally be in the physical presence of our Lord and Savior, Jesus Christ. After a first date like that, of course we will want to experience more and more of His presence. The Heavenly Romance starts out with a significant milestone. We have our first date with our beloved Savior. We dine in the midst of the Paradise of God. We eat from His hand the most delicious and nutritious meal in all of the universe. This romance is off to a grand start. It makes you wonder what comes next, right? Well, keep on reading. It gets better moving forward.

"Going Steady"

Revelation 2:17

*"He who has an ear, let him hear what the Spirit says to the churches. To him who overcomes I will give some of the **hidden manna** to eat. And I will give him **a white stone**, and on the stone **a new name** written which no one knows except him who receives it."*

There comes a time in any budding romance when the relationship moves beyond dating. Both parties agree that things are going well. The experience is mutually rewarding. The warm and fuzzy feelings are still there. True characters are revealed; loving bonds grow stronger. Exclusivity becomes an effortless delight, rather than a begrudging obligation. There are no other persons of interest. No one else occupies the thoughts and imaginations. In some romances the transition can be pinpointed to a specific time and place. In others it happens over time, almost imperceptibly. Some couples make formal declarations of commitment to each other. Others make quiet assumptions that things have moved to the next level.

(**Note:** I was always more comfortable with the formal declaration of my intentions. Of course, there was always a moment or two of uneasiness as I waited for a positive response. Over time I adopted a policy: I would never make a declaration of that magnitude unless I knew what the response would be. I needed to be, at least, 99% certain that the response would be a favorable one. Even then, it only worked out in my favor about 50% of the time ... Sigh.)

In any event, there are signposts indicating that the relationship has reached a new level of intimacy. One of those markers is the giving of meaningful gifts. In our passage (Rev. 2:17), we see Christ promising three special gifts to His beloved. Let's take a look at each of these unique gifts and their significance.

"Hidden Manna"

We first became aware of the word "manna" back in the book of Exodus. The children of Israel woke up one morning to find it covering the ground. They had no idea what it was, and so they called it "manna." Moses told them that it was the bread that the LORD had provided for them to eat. So, for forty years that's what they ate. Exodus 16:31 describes manna this way "… *and it was like coriander seed, white; and the taste of it was like wafers made with honey."* Upon researching images of coriander seeds, I wasn't too impressed. But, if it tasted like "wafers made with honey," then the word "yummy" immediately comes to my mind. Honey is sweet

and it has many health benefits. All over the world honey has value.

There are dozens upon dozens of different types of wafers. They come in many different shapes, sizes, and flavors. Wafers are light, crisp, and delicious. Even though we don't know exactly what the manna looked like or even tasted like, we do know that it was white. We know that it was like coriander seed, and it tasted like honey-flavored wafers. There must have been an amazing amount of nutritional value in them as well. Manna was the primary source of sustenance for the Israelites for forty years. So, it must have been both delicious and nutritious.

Now, let's clear up one small thing about manna. Apparently, in the time of the New Testament, some people described manna as "the bread of Heaven." But, when Jesus was given the opportunity, He had the following explanation: *"I am the bread of life. Your fathers ate the manna in the wilderness, and are dead. This is the bread which comes down from heaven that one may eat of it and not die. I am the living bread which came down from heaven. If anyone eats of this bread, he will live forever; and the bread that I shall give is My flesh, which I shall give for the life of the world"* (John 6:48–51).

So, manna is a very delicious-sounding, nutritionally-balanced food. God prepared it especially for His people when they needed it most. But, it is not the "Bread of Heaven."

There is an interesting side note to the manna narrative in Exodus 16:33. *"And Moses said to Aaron, 'Take a pot and put an omer of manna in it, and lay it up before the LORD, to be kept for your generations.'"*

Aaron apparently did as he was told. Generations later we read about it in the New Testament. The author of Hebrews describes the earthly tabernacle and its contents: *"which had the golden censer and the ark of the covenant overlaid on all sides with gold, in which were the **golden pot that had the manna**, Aaron's rod that* *budded, and the tablets of the covenant"* (Hebrews 9:4).

The next time there is any mention of manna in the Bible, it is in our text. Jesus promises to give some of it to His love interest. "... *I will give some of the **hidden manna** to eat.*" Can you see it in your imagination?

One day you and Jesus are walking through Heaven and Jesus says He has a surprise for you. He then takes you by the hand and hurriedly leads you off to a secluded section of the heavenly garden. He stops in a remote corner where there is a cluster of flowers. Hidden behind the beautiful flowers is a golden treasure chest. The chest is enclosed in a crystal case. He expertly reaches into the case and removes the chest. He sets it down and motions for you to join Him as He takes a seat on the grass. He opens the chest revealing several priceless objects.

Each object has eternal significance. The Law of the Covenant, written with

God's own finger, is in there. The rod of Aaron, which is still alive after all these millennia, is in there. Then, there is a golden pot. Christ tenderly takes out the pot. His excitement is evident as He smiles knowingly at what you are about to experience. As He removes the lid from the pot, the sweetest aroma fills the atmosphere. The scent is intoxicating—in fact, it's more than just a smell. It is like nothing you have ever experienced before. The aroma seems to totally envelop you, like a warm hug.

Jesus reaches into the pot and just before pulling His hand out He asks you to close your eyes and open your mouth. With complete trust, you obey His request. You close your eyes and open your mouth. You experience the most exquisite sensation. Your tongue is treated to the sweetest delicacy in all Heaven. Instinctively, you open your eyes and let out a prolonged "Mmmmm! It's Dee-licious!" You know that it is manna. It tastes even better than your wildest imagination could have ever dreamed it would be. Jesus smiles lovingly, knowing that He has saved this piece of manna just for you. He hid it away, for eons, and looked forward to the very moment when you would taste it for the first time. That's what lovers do. They plan surprises that will warm the heart of their loved one. Hidden manna ... what an awesome surprise gift!

"A White Stone"

The second gift that Christ gives us is a precious white stone. "... *And I will give him a white stone...*"

There are many significant stones mentioned in the Bible:

- David picked up five, smooth stones on his way to fight Goliath.
- Jacob used a stone as a pillow the night that he saw the ladder and wrestled with God.

- God wrote the Ten Commandments on tablets of stone.
- The children of Israel took up stones as they crossed through the Jordan River.

Stones seemed to always bear significant meaning. Many of the stories involving Jesus also had stones in them:

- Satan tempted Jesus to turn stones into bread.
- Jesus' first miracle involved six stone pots that were filled with water that He turned into wine.
- The leaders in the temple tried to stone Jesus on more than one occasion.
- The woman caught in adultery heard the sound of stones falling to the ground as she knelt at the feet of Jesus.
- Jesus commanded that the stone be rolled away from the tomb of Lazarus.

- Jesus referred to Himself as the "stone that the builders rejected."
- The stone that covered Jesus' tomb was rolled away before the disciples arrived on Resurrection Sunday morning.

There are so many different sizes, types, uses, and descriptions for stones. It is interesting to note that there is only one reference to white stones in the whole Bible. That reference is in our text, Revelation 2:17.

The manna is left over from the Exodus. But, this white stone that Jesus gives to us will be a brand-new stone. It has never been used for any other purpose. No one else has owned it or worn it. It has been made especially for you and for me. It is an

Each is a one-of-a-kind creation. No two are the same. Christ presents this gift to His lover in the tenderest manner.

exclusive. Each is a one-of-a-kind creation. No two are the same. Christ presents this gift to His lover in the tenderest manner. Whether He places it in your hand or slides it onto your wrist, or finger, we will have to wait to find out. Maybe He has it attached to a chain of gold and places it around your neck. What matters most is that it is a gift from one Lover to another. So, its value is priceless. You will never be without it. It is something tangible that you will carry with you all the time, wherever you go.

That is what lovers do. They give special gifts to each other. The gifts often represent certain milestones in their

relationship. The gifts are valued more than the actual price of the materials used to create them. There is sentimental value attached to the gift that no amount of money could replace. It is unique; it is irreplaceable. It is *priceless*.

I look forward to getting my white stone. How about you? Do you yearn for your stone? It will be a cherished keepsake for all of eternity. But like they say in late-night advertisements… "But wait, there's more!"

As you hold the stone in your hand, examining it from every angle, you notice something. What you see on your stone is absolutely wonderful. The stone is engraved with a word that makes you smile from ear to ear and maybe even blush a bit.

"A New Name"

The third gift comes as an added surprise with a uniquely personal touch.

"...a new name written which no one knows except him who receives it."

When I was younger, I thought that it would be kind of cool to find out my "new name." I was under the impression that my name would be changed in the same manner that Abram became Abraham. Jacob became Israel. Saul became Paul. It would be a dramatic and visible declaration that I was now a citizen of the heavenly kingdom. Each of us would have these new names. We would walk around heaven re-introducing ourselves to everyone else. Everyone would know our new names.

Boy, was I wrong!

In our text, we read about the third gift that Jesus presents to us. It signifies that our dating relationship is transitioning to something even more meaningful. As you examine gift number two, the white stone, you notice an inscription. You blush at the sight of it. It is a name that Jesus only uses when He is speaking to you, in your most tender moments with Him. It is not a name that He calls you in public. It is very private. You know the type of name. We use similar names here on Earth. Here are a few examples, in random order:

- Sugar Plum
- Sweet Cheeks
- Honey Bear
- Muffin
- Cherry Blossom
- Cuddles
- Bubbles
- Honey Bunch
- Love Bug
- Cutie Pie
- Sunshine
- Chicken Nugget
- Peaches
- Pudding
- Sugar Dumpling
- Tater-Tot

The list could go on and on. We call them "pet names." They often are related to some

"Going Steady" *(Revelation 2:17)*

kind of tasty treat, or warm, fuzzy animal or a combination of the two. The words by themselves seem to elicit pleasant thoughts. But when associated with a person, the words take on even greater significance.

Lovers use these names in private, when they are talking to one another. Often, the name is so special that it is only uttered in hushed tones. Sometimes, they share their pet name with others that are very close to them. But, the name is definitely NOT for public use. It is a name that only the lover and the loved one know.

It is a name that only the lover and the loved one know.

So, I was wrong. I thought that my new name would be known by all. I thought that I would proudly use it to introduce myself to the other inhabitants of heaven. As it turns out, it is a name that Jesus will give me that I will guard as closely as I guard my white stone.

What a sweet surprise gift we will receive from our Precious Savior!

You know the relationship has reached a higher level when you start using pet names. After a while, though, the relationship reaches another turning point. It is the point where it's time to make a formal commitment, and move on to the next phase. Typically, the man asks a question and the woman gives a response. If the response is a positive one (YES!), then the couple is "engaged to be married."

What does that look like in our "Heavenly Romance" with Jesus?

Well, let's pick up our story in the last part of Revelation, chapter 2.

"The Engagement"

Revelation 2:26–28

*"And he who overcomes, and keeps My works until the end, to him I will give **power over the nations**—'He shall rule them with a rod of iron; They shall be dashed to pieces like the potter's vessels'—as I also have received from My Father; and I will give him **the morning star**."*

It's time to "pop the question," as the saying goes. Usually, the guy is the one who does the "popping" after taking a posture of vulnerability. Down on one knee, he reaches into his pocket and pulls out a small, yet precious, box. His voice trembles as he makes eye contact with the love of his life. The woman, filled with surprise, anticipation, and watery eyes, stops breathing. He speaks (and sometimes, squeaks) the words to the question that she's been waiting to hear all her life: "Will you marry me?" His words hang in the air like an iridescent soap bubble on a balmy afternoon in Southern California. He opens the box, revealing a sparkling jewel. The sight of the jewel elicits a gasp from the woman (she needed to breathe, anyway). He stretches out the box to her, and she knows that by accepting the offering, she is also answering his question.

This scenario has been rehearsed in her mind on many occasions. But, when the real thing happens, it still feels surreal.

"The Engagement" *(Revelation 2:26–28)* † 53

She nods her head, up and down. The word comes out, as a stuttered whisper … "Y-y-yes" … then a confident declaration … "Yes" … and finally an emphatic, joy-filled shout … "YES!!" Her excitement is unleashed. She dances a little dance as he takes her trembling left hand. He places the contents of the little box on her ring finger. She extends her hand as far from her body as she can (Is she far-sighted? … or is she showing it off to all who are around? I'm not quite sure why women do that thing) and examines and admires the gem from every angle.

Meanwhile, he rises to his feet, studying her facial expression and body language. He can't help but ask the question, "So, do you like it?" Her emotional response brings him a combination of emotions. He feels relief, joy, and a sense of accomplishment. "I love it" she declares. "It's perfect." In essence, he is offering her much more than the diamond ring. The ring represents his undying love and devotion for her. He is offering himself totally to his one, true love. All that he has, and all that he is, he offers to her in the symbol of that precious gem.

We have watched that scene play out countless times in the movies, or on TV. We have read about it in romance novels. (Now, when I say "we", I don't necessarily mean "me." But, you know who you are if those statements apply to you … wink, wink). That is exactly how the script is written. It is supposed to play out that way. It is what we have grown to expect. In fact, when things don't work out that way, it surprises us, right?

Well, in our text for today (Rev. 2:28), Christ promises to give us something priceless, rare, and sparkly. Of course, since it is Christ giving the gift we know that it is going to be extra special. The gem that He presents to us can't be purchased at the mall or even a fancy jewelry store. You can't find it in the diamond mines of Africa or anywhere on Earth, for that matter. If you search for the term "Morning Star," you will find that that is the term given to the planet Venus. As seen from Earth, Venus appears in the eastern sky. It appears brighter, in fact, than any of the stars in the sky, even though it is a planet. But, I doubt that is the "Morning Star" that Jesus is speaking about.

Maybe, there is a star that we haven't seen yet; in fact it may be a star that God creates for us* on that special day. There is a third option, however, that I find the

---

*Many years ago, a special friend of mine gave me a star for my birthday. Yes, a star! Apparently, there is an organization that gives each star a numerical designation, after plotting its place in the heavens. There are many stars that have been given these designations. So, a person can actually contact the organization and request a star be assigned to them. The person receives a certificate with the coordinates of the star's location. They also receive the star's numerical designation. By the way, I have no idea where my certificate is; neither do I remember the coordinates of my star's location. But, somewhere, up there, is my star.

most likely and also the most appealing. The only other place that the term "Morning Star" appears in the Bible is also in the book of Revelation. We find it in chapter 22, verse 16: *"I, Jesus, have sent My angel to testify to you these things in the churches. I am the Root and the Offspring of David, the Bright and **Morning Star**."*

Did you catch that? Jesus says that **He IS the Morning Star**. Oh, how exciting! So, Jesus offers us all that He is, all that He has, everything! He gets down on one knee, He stretches out His nail-pierced hands, and He says to you, and He says to me, "I offer Myself to you. Will you have Me?" No matter how often we may rehearse this scene in our minds, I can only imagine that some of us may stutter a bit as we answer. Our mouths quiver as we form the words "y—y-yes, I will have You. I love You. You are perfect!"

I don't know about you, but maybe—just maybe—I will break out in a little dance.

There is another promise stated in the first part of the text (Rev. 2:26), "*...to him I will give **power over the nations**.*" This makes perfect sense when you think about it. Jesus has authority over the entire universe. When He extends His hands to us, offering Himself to us, He is also offering all that He owns. He offers not only the tangible, physical attributes of His kingdom, but He also offers the authority that comes with His rule. We will actually share in His dominion over all things.

One of the benefits of being in a committed relationship is shared authority. A woman can ward off a pesky salesman, even when her husband isn't with her. She can say, "Well, let me speak with my husband first, then WE will get back to you." In another example, the man could be out in the marketplace and notice something that is special and unique. He knows his wife would love to have it. He can buy the item, and then present it to her later.

It is something that she would have missed out on if he had not come across it. When two become one, there is a distinct advantage because now they have shared authority. Each one has the authority to act on the other's behalf. Anything that is against one of them has to now face both of them. Neither one stands alone ... ever. Imagine being linked to Christ in such a special manner.

One of the benefits of being in a committed relationship is shared authority.

Jesus offers to give us power to crush any and all enemies of His. Before this, in our life on Earth, we didn't have the power to stand against evil on our own. We had to call upon the name of Jesus for help to deliver us from the snares of the enemy. Now, we will be given power to "…[dash them] to pieces…like the potter's vessels." Sin and evil will never rise again. Our shared authority with Christ, within this Holy Engagement, has profound benefits. It ensures that nothing, or no one, will come between us and our Beloved ever again!

"The Ceremony"

Revelation 3:5

*"He who overcomes shall be clothed in **white garments**, and I will **not blot***

*out his name from the Book of Life; but I will **confess his name before My Father** and before His angels."*

The time of the engagement has reached its zenith. It is now time to get married. The wedding day has arrived. It is time for the ceremony. This day has been highly anticipated. There is no nervousness or anxiety to mar the occasion. It is with unblemished delight and unbridled joy that we welcome the day of our marriage to the Lamb of God. The Heavenly hosts are gathered together. The venue is exquisitely decorated. The music is grand and glorious. Amidst all of the unimaginable pomp and circumstance that will take place, there are certain elements that stand out.* Isn't that also the case in our current weddings? It is nice to

---

*My definition of a wedding. A legally binding exchange of vows, between a man and a woman, in the presence of one or more witnesses, with no one objecting.

have white doves, the horse drawn carriage, and the latest "wedding song" sung by the original artist. But when you peel away those nice touches, there are more important things that must take place. Our text mentions three critical elements that will happen on that glorious day. It is the day of our Heavenly Wedding Ceremony.

"White Garments"

Nothing says "wedding ceremony" like white garments. The color white represents purity and innocence. It symbolizes truth and light, honesty and transparency. Cleanliness and holiness are also depicted using the color white. It also denotes a fresh start—something brand new. So, the significance of white garments is clear. We will wear garments that represent all that is pure and holy. As the song says: "Here comes the bride, all dressed in **white**…"

There is an even deeper meaning associated with these white garments, though.

"The Ceremony" (Revelation 3:5)

The garments represent the righteousness of Christ, Himself! Without Christ's righteousness, we wouldn't even be allowed to enter into this Heavenly Romance. In fact, we would not be in heaven, at all. There would be no wedding ceremony.

Further along in the book of Revelation, we find out how the robes got to be white in the first place. *"These are the ones who come out of the great tribulation, and washed their robes and **made them white in the blood of the Lamb**"* (Rev. 7:14). It is literally, the blood of Jesus Christ that makes our robes white. What a privilege and an honor to be clothed in the righteousness of Christ! Putting on that white garment will elicit unspeakable humility. Profound and unrestrained joy will burst forth. I can even imagine that I will do a little twirl, in the robe, once I have it on. How about you?

> What a privilege and an honor to be clothed in the righteousness of Christ!

In vivid contrast to our joyous wedding ceremony, there is a story recorded in the book of Matthew, chapter 22. Jesus tells a parable of a wedding ceremony. In the story one of the guests shows up **without** the proper wedding garment. When the host of the wedding feast, the King, approaches and asks the question, "Friend, how did you come in here without a wedding garment?" … the man is speechless (v. 12). The proverbial cat got his proverbial tongue. He provides no explanation or rational excuse. There is nothing that he can say that will make the situation any better. So he remains silent. But, his silence doesn't last long.

The King then turns to his servants and pronounces judgment. *"Bind him hand and foot, take him away, and cast him into outer darkness; there will be **weeping and gnashing of teeth**"* (v. 13). That man did not get to enjoy the pleasures and excitement of the wedding celebration. He was to be tied up and dragged out. Then he faced being

"The Ceremony" *(Revelation 3:5)* † 65

cast into "outer darkness," no doubt, full of remorse, regret, and pain. Off in the distance, you can almost hear his whimpering and weeping.

The Word of God makes it clear that the white garment is of supreme value. With it, we have access to the glorious splendor of paradise, forever. Without it, we face painful agony and total destruction. Let us look forward with anticipation to that day when the white robe is draped over our shoulders. It will lovingly be placed on us by the One who made it all possible by willingly shedding His blood.

"The Book of Life"

The next element that is mentioned in the text is this statement, made by Jesus: "*...I will **not blot out his/(her) name from the Book of Life**...*" Wow! That sounds important doesn't it? The only way that a name could be "blotted out" of the book of life, is if it is already written in the book of life. So, the good news is, that our names are already written there. This makes sense because we are wearing the white robes (The Righteousness of Christ). This means that we have already been granted eternal life. The second fact is that, at least, at some point, the ceremony could have been cancelled. Your name or my name could have been blotted out. But, since we've reached this part of the ceremony, then that won't happen. Jesus makes that clear.

Okay, so what exactly is the book of life? Well, the book of life is the official document that contains the names of every man, woman, boy, and girl who has submitted their will to Jesus Christ. They have allowed Him to put the white robe of His righteousness on them. They are the ones who have washed their robes in the blood of the Lamb.

Note: There are eight passages in the Bible that mention the Book of Life. In each text, it is made clear that those whose names are written in that book are in good shape. In contrast, those whose names are not written in the book of life are on the wrong side of heaven. The clearest text on the subject is Revelation 20:15: *"And anyone not found written in the Book of Life was cast into the lake of fire."*

Having your name written in the Lamb's book of life is of utmost importance. It is more important than being on any guest list, here on Earth. It is more important than the Hall of Fame or a "Who's Who" list. Why? ... Because, it is evidence that all of your sins have been blotted out. It is evidence that you stand before God clothed in the righteousness of His Son, Jesus Christ.

So, when Jesus declares "…I will **not blot out his** [or her] **name from the Book of Life**," He is vowing eternal commitment and connection. Nothing will be able to tear asunder our union to Him. Our earthly ceremonies contain the words "until death do us part." There are no such stipulations in our marriage to the Lamb. When Christ speaks His vows, there are no qualifying clauses. Death will be no more. No sickness, only health. No poverty, only wealth. So, there is nothing that can separate us from our Beloved Savior.

"Confession"

The third crucial element of the ceremony is a declaration, made by Jesus. "…I will **confess his** [or her] **name before My Father** and before His angels." What is the text telling us? What is the significance of this statement? Well, another definition of the word "confess" in this passage is "profess." To profess means to declare, announce, proclaim, assert, state, affirm, maintain, or avow. We've heard pastors, priests, and judges make similar announcements at the end of wedding ceremonies. "Ladies and Gentlemen, I now present to you Mr. and Mrs. So and So." It is a grand moment when the official proclamation is made. It marks the end of the formal ceremony. It is the introduction of the newly formed union to the rest of the world. It is the first time that the bride is officially called by her husband's name.

Our Savior doesn't delegate this privilege to anyone else in the whole universe. He makes the joyous announcement Himself. So, what Christ is saying in the text, is that He will make the formal and public declaration that He is now married to you. He will make the announcement before the God of the universe and all who are in attendance. He will proclaim in a loud voice that we are His and He is ours.

I can only imagine what kind of exuberant shouts of joy and songs of congratulations will burst froth from the Heavenly hosts! It will be amazing! ... and God, our Father, will smile.

"The Marriage"

Revelation 3:12, 21

"*He who overcomes, I will make him a pillar in the temple of My God, and he shall go out no more. I will write on him the name of My God and the name of the city of My God, the New Jerusalem, which comes down out of heaven from My God: and I will write on him My new name.*"

> *"To him who overcomes I will grant to **sit with Me on My throne**, as I also overcame and sat down with My Father on His throne."*

I have often been asked the question, "Which is more important—getting married or staying married?" My answer has been, "It depends. It's most important to get married, if you are not married. It's most important to stay married, once you've gotten married."

Well, now the wedding ceremony is over. It was the wedding ceremony of all ceremonies. Nothing could have been grander! The whole universe attended. Now, it's time for the marriage relationship to swing into full force. Sadly, for many marriages, it goes downhill after the wedding. It has even been observed that some couples end their marriage before the wedding is completely paid off. SMH (Shaking My Head, for those of you who don't speak text—LOL).

Certain realities start to dawn on the young couple, whose cheeks are still sore from all the smiling. Someone has to do the cooking and cleaning. Someone has to work extra hours to afford the new house and all the bills. Who is going to do the laundry, the dishes, the yard work? As time goes on, someone has to get up to change the baby. Then, who is going to pick the kids up from school and take them to soccer practice? Whose idea was it to have three kids in the first place? Why do we always go to your parents for Thanksgiving? On and on it goes and sometimes it seems to be overwhelming. One partner begins to feel neglected or taken for granted. The slightest thing can seem like a personal attack. Before too long, papers are signed, the U-Haul® is loaded, and the marriage has ended.

"A Pillar"

That will not be the case at all in this Heavenly Romance. There will be no bills, no headaches, no fear or insecurity. Jesus, Himself, has conquered sin, and death. He has utterly destroyed all our enemies. No tears, or failures or misunderstandings will invade the Holy environment of Heaven. We will be free from all harm and hurt feelings. We will be free to sing and dance with Jesus!

The very atmosphere will be full of love, freedom, and peace. All the "over comers" will experience uninterrupted bliss. Joy will be our constant emotion. No one will want to leave. The notion of packing up and going somewhere else won't exist. None will be disgruntled. Jesus promises to make us *"a pillar in the temple"* and we *"shall go out no more."*

That sounds like the marriage is intended to be permanent. There is no hint of wandering or straying away. Pillars don't move. They support the rest of the structure. Pillars don't leave the building. The beloved of God won't leave His presence. We will be living the dream. Remember David, in Psalm 27:4? He said:

> *"One thing I have desired of the LORD, That will I seek: That I may dwell in the house of the LORD All the days of my life, To behold the beauty of the LORD, And to inquire in His temple."*

Well, there it is. Dream fulfilled.

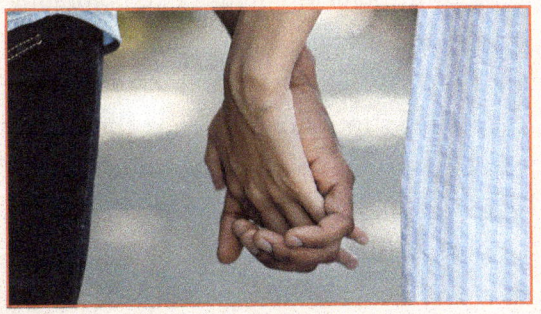

"A Tattoo"

Next, we read that Jesus is going to give us a tattoo. That's right, **a tattoo**. In fact, the text gives us some details about this unique tattoo. It will contain three special names: the name of God, the name of the City (New Jerusalem), and the new name of Jesus. Can you imagine that? What will it look like? What kind of ink will He use? Where is He going to put the tattoo? What is going to be the new name of Jesus? So many questions! And, what is the significance of these three names?

Well, it sounds to me like the tattoo will represent themes. Themes like belonging, residence, and union. We belong to God, we reside in His temple, and we are forever joined to Christ. Tattoos these days often represent some of the same themes, right? People have tattoos with the names or images of loved ones. Others have the name of their place of birth or land of citizenship tattooed on their body. I've also seen the names and/or logos of favorite sports teams. Some tattoos are artistic patterns or designs. Some people are covered with lots of "ink" as part of their persona. Tattoos have become a method of personal expression for many.

Then there are many people (like myself) who would never, ever even consider getting a tattoo. For one reason or another, the thought is not appealing. Some don't do it because it is forbidden by their parents. Others are afraid of the possible pain. Still others are not able to commit to anything that seems permanent. Yet others simply like the way they look without any markings on their body.

In the Heavenly Romance, we will welcome the tattoo that Christ offers to give us. We will be honored and pleased to accept the markings. There will be no fear of pain. No one will forbid it. The permanence that it represents will be part of the joyful covenant. Everyone will be forever reminded that we belong to God's family.

Our residence in His holy temple in the New Jerusalem will never be a question. We will forever be citizens of His kingdom.

To top it all off, Jesus will reveal to us His new name! Whoa…! What could it be? Why does *He* need a new name? I'm curious to find out … aren't you? How curiously exciting! We are not told what His new name will be. But, we read that He will write His new name on us. Oh, what a thrill! We will have the name of our Beloved etched onto our being, in such permanent fashion. What an intimate reminder of Who we belong to.

That is the one tattoo that I look forward to receiving.

"The Throne"

There is no higher position than the throne of God. It can't get any better than that. It is the seat of all power, majesty, authority, glory, and dominion. It is the center of the Universe! He who sits on the throne of God is the Alpha and the Omega, the beginning and the end. Everything that was made, was made by Him. Jesus sits on that throne. There is no name above the name of Jesus. So isn't it amazing that He invites us to sit on the throne with Him? We will share in the majesty and dominion that belongs to Him. We are His bride; we are joint heirs of the promise. We are children of the Most High God. We will take our rightful place, right next to Christ, sitting on His throne. What an awesome privilege and honor! 1 Corinthians 6:3 states: *"Do you not know that we shall judge angels?"* Isn't that incredible?!

What a long way we have come! In Psalms we read: *"What is man that You are mindful of him, And the son of man that You*

visit him? For You have made him a little lower than the angels, And You have crowned him with glory and honor" (8:4, 5). Although we started out "a little lower than the angels," being married to Christ places us in a position to "judge angels." We cannot begin to fathom all the implications. Our minds cannot comprehend all the benefits of this Heavenly Romance. In fact, the Holy Bible says in 1 Corinthians 2:9 "***…Eye has not seen, nor ear heard, Nor have entered into the heart of man The things which God has prepared for those who love Him.***"

We will share the throne of God, and dwell in the presence of our Beloved Savior, for eternity. No worry, no fear, no sorrow, pain, or death will mar our existence. We will reign with Jesus in perfect peace, love, and harmony. Saints and angels will be our constant companions. What could be better than this? Well that's actually a great question. The answer may surprise you. Check out the next chapter, entitled: "The Beginning."

"The Beginning"

1 Corinthians 2:9

"…Eye has not seen, nor ear heard, nor have entered into the heart of man the things which God has prepared for those who love Him."

Can you imagine what Heaven will be like? Can you imagine what eternity feels like? Do you have any idea what we will be doing for eternity, in the presence of God? Have you ever wondered what form of travel we will use? What language will be spoken? Other than the tree of life, in the midst of the garden of God, what will we eat? What kinds of plants, animals, smells, and sights will we discover? How tall will you be? Will I finally be able to sing well? How will it feel to not have night time?

We've all seen pictures depicting heaven. We have heard stories about what heaven will be like from the time we were small. We have even read passages in the Bible that describe what others have witnessed in visions. So, at some point, we may feel that we have a pretty good idea about heaven. But, when we read a text like 1 Corinthians 2:9, it gives us a much better perspective. Actually, it gives us the best point of view.

If your imagination can answer any of the above questions, then you have it wrong. The most beautiful sights that you have seen don't even come close to what

God has prepared for you. The best paintings, sculptures, waterfalls, rainbows, constellations, flowers, birds, butterflies, are pale imitations. Think of the most moving melody, or harmonious voices, you've ever heard. You might believe that the music from the heavenly choirs will sound like that. You'd be wrong. We have never heard anything like the sounds we will hear in heaven.

Sometimes I'm fascinated when I see a science fiction TV show or movie. The creative landscapes and creatures that the writers and directors create are amazing. They have taken images that existed only in their imaginations and brought them to the screen. Scenes that lived only in their minds are now shared with the world. I've often wondered, "How did they come up with that?" When I watch a documentary about the making of the movie or TV show, the author will often share how he came up with the ideas and images. He or she will explain how something they saw or heard reminded them of something else. They will describe how the unique sights and sounds were created. They explain how bits and pieces of certain elements are taken apart. And then those pieces are simply put together in different ways.

One thing becomes quite clear to me. They have taken something that is familiar and created something new. The ingredients are rearranged in unique ways to create illusions. They add to or subtract from what is usual, and that creates something unusual. Once we take a look "behind the scenes" we can see exactly how they did it.

That will not be the case in Heaven. God is not going to shuffle the cards, creating the illusion that all things are new. He is THE Creator! He creates. His imagination is limitless. He creates all the time. There is never a time when He isn't creating. Do you believe the colors and hues that the human eye can see are the only colors in the universe? Is it possible that there are sounds that God has not shared with us yet? Are there smells that don't exist in our solar system? Are there sensations and feelings that we can only experience in the atmosphere of heaven? These are some interesting questions. Here are a few more:

> What if it were possible to hear colors?
> Can sounds have a smell to them?
> Do our eyes have the ability to see fragrances?

I don't have the answer to any of those questions, but, guess what? God has the answers to those questions and many, many more. Beyond that, He has even more questions than you or I could ever ask ... more than all humanity could ever conceive. Ask Brother Job from the Old Testament (see Job chapters 38–41). In that passage, God is asking questions that Job never dreamed of asking. These are questions that never even entered Job's imagination. So, God has the answers to all our questions before we even ask them. His wisdom and knowledge are limitless. In fact, wisdom and knowledge do not exist outside of God. He is the source of all truth. He is the author of all wisdom. There is no idea, concept, or creative design that He is not aware of. Nothing surprises Him. He knows it all, because He made it all.

So, God has the answers to all our questions before we even ask them. His wisdom and knowledge are limitless.

Scientists and researchers will tell you that there are no two snowflakes that are alike. No two grains of sand or blades of grass are identical. Can you imagine that? Can you imagine the amount of creativity it takes to come up with different designs for gazillions times gazillions of snowflakes? God's creativity goes far beyond anything that we could even imagine. In fact, if He described some of the surprises He has prepared for us in heaven, we wouldn't be able to comprehend them. What if an automobile designer/engineer tried to explain the inner workings of a car to a two-year old? How much of his thorough and detailed description would the child understand? That's why the author of 1 Corinthians didn't even try to describe what we would encounter when we get to heaven. We couldn't imagine or understand it, even if God described it to us. How do you describe a color that no one has ever seen before?

We can't accurately describe what heaven is going to be like, can we? So, how can we fully describe how our marriage to the Lamb will play out? We have glimpses into the future. We have a lot of information about what will NOT be there. No sin, no pain, no sorrow, no fear, no strife, no misunderstanding, no disappointment. For many people, the absence of anything negative is enough. But, for many others (like myself), there needs to be more. Some of us want to know what will we do? Who will be there? How will we travel from place to place?

There is a part of me that wishes we had the answer to all those questions right now. Then, there is another part of me that loves a great mystery. A part of me longs to be involved in a true adventure. A part of me wants to have a role in the best romance story of all time. I want my name to be joined with the rest of the names included in this story.

The Heavenly Romance concludes with these words:

And they lived happily, ever after!
The Beginning...

TEACH Services, Inc.
P U B L I S H I N G
www.TEACHServices.com • (800) 367-1844

We invite you to view the complete
selection of titles we publish at:
www.TEACHServices.com

We encourage you to write us
with your thoughts about this,
or any other book we publish at:
info@TEACHServices.com

TEACH Services' titles may be purchased
in bulk quantities for educational, fund-
raising, business, or promotional use.
bulksales@TEACHServices.com

Finally, if you are interested in seeing
your own book in print, please contact us
at: **publishing@TEACHServices.com**

We are happy to review your manuscript
at no charge.

www.ingramcontent.com/pod-product-compliance
Lightning Source LLC
Chambersburg PA
CBHW070558160426
43199CB00014B/2546